IT'S NOT OVER YET

How and where to get help when you have hit rock bottom and don't know what else to do

Naomy Mburu

KINGDOM BOOKS
Your kingdom come, your will be done

Copyright © Naomy Mburu, 2016

Published by Kingdom Books, an imprint of *CreativeJuicesBooks, Singapore (www.creativejuicesbooks.com)*

All rights reserved. No part of this book may be reproduced, stored in a retrieval system, or transmitted in any form or by any means—electronic, mechanical, digital, photocopy, recording, or any other—except for brief quotations in printed reviews, without prior permission in writing from the publisher.

All Scripture quotations, unless otherwise indicated, are taken from the *Holy Bible: New King James Version®*. Copyright © 1982 by Thomas Nelson. Used by permission. All rights reserved.

Scripture quotations marked *NIV* are taken from the *Holy Bible: New International Version ®*. Copyright © 1973, 1978, 1984 International Bible Society. Used by permission of Zondervan Bible Publishers. All rights reserved.

Scripture quotations marked *KJV* are taken from the *Holy Bible: King James Version*.

Scripture quotations marked *TLB* are taken from *The Living Bible* copyright © 1971. Used by permission of Tyndale House Publishers, Inc., Carol Stream, Illinois 60188. All rights reserved.

Scripture quotations marked *AMP* are taken from the *Amplified® Bible*, copyright © 1954, 1958, 1962, 1964, 1965, 1987 by The Lockman Foundation. Used by permission.

Scripture quotations marked *MSG* are taken from *The Message*. Copyright © 1993, 1994, 1995, 1996, 2000, 2001, 2002. Used by permission of NavPress Publishing Group.

National Library Board, Singapore Cataloguing-in-Publication Data
Name(s): Mburu, Naomy.
Title: It's not over yet: how and where to get help when you have hit rock bottom and don't know what else to do / Naomy Mburu.
Other title(s): How and where to get help when you have hit rock bottom and don't know what else to do
Description: Singapore: Kingdom Books, [2016]
Identifier(s): OCN 957706225 | ISBN 978-981-11-0388-9 (paperback)
Subject(s): LCSH: Trust in God. | God (Christianity)--Promises. | Christian life.
Classification: DDC 248.48--dc23

Contents

Acknowledgments — iv

Introduction — 1

1. The Power of Your Tongue — 5
2. Remember Past Victories — 21
3. Do Not Listen to Negative Voices — 34
4. Sing Praises to God — 49
5. Keep a Positive Mindset — 57
6. Be Joyful Always — 70
7. Belief Backed by Action is Powerful — 80
8. Learn to Forgive — 91
9. Be Disciplined — 99

Acknowledgments

To God the Almighty, who has seen me through every single struggle in my life, and who has made me come out victorious and stronger than before—all glory and honor to your name, my Father.

To my loving husband Yaah—my love, you have been the best thing that ever happened to me. Your love, friendship, kindness and patience have made me a better person. I can confidently say life has been worth living with you by my side. Thanks for believing in me and continuously inspiring me to move forward. You have made me discover that I can do anything I set my mind to. There are no words to thank you; I simply say, "I love you."

To Ryan and Xavier—I know you are too young to understand this, my sons, but believe me when I say that just looking at your faces gives me a great deal of motivation. Thank you for coming into my life.

To Lynn, Queen and Tracy—you are simply amazing. You mean a lot to me. Thanks for believing in this book; your input and dedication to this project have been outstanding. I cannot thank you enough.

To the many people who have contributed to make this book possible—thank you, and may God bless you for being of great help in my life.

Introduction

It is no secret that all of us pass through tough times at one point or another. During these difficult seasons of our lives, we tend to blame ourselves, others or even God for the hardships we are going through. But always remember this: no matter how tough it gets, God will never abandon you.

One thing we can be sure of is that hard times do not determine who we will be in the future. They are not death sentences for us. If we stay in faith and refuse to be defeated, God will always make a way—even where there is no way.

It is important to keep your focus on God no matter how stormy it gets in your life. Our God does not change. He is still God no matter what happens. Tough times do not change God. Once you discover that, you will learn to trust Him even more. You will shift your focus from your problems to the greatness of our God and His ability to deliver you from those problems.

Maybe your health is failing you, and it seems like there is nothing else left for you to do—other than to wait for your impending death. But take heart; the Bible says that by His stripes we are healed (*1 Peter 2:24*). Believe in Jesus and trust Him to carry all your burdens and make you whole again.

In this book, I will show you step by step how to focus on becoming better in every area of your life. I will guide you to keep moving forward, even when the forces that come against you seem so overpowering. I will reveal to you simple, effective ways of getting yourself out of seemingly hopeless situations. These simple steps have worked wonders in my own life. So keep believing in yourself and, with God's help, you will definitely be better off than you are now.

It is true that sometimes God allows us to go through hard times so that we can learn to rely entirely on Him, and not on our own understanding. One thing we can be sure of is that God does not want us to remain trapped in the predicament we are in. He wants us to use the ammunition He has given us to get ourselves out of those terrible situations.

The enemy on the other hand wants us to remain down there—beaten, frustrated and defeated. Friend, you do not have to accept any of that. Always fight back. The Bible says that our

Introduction

struggle is against the principalities and rulers of darkness (*Ephesians 6:12*), who constantly try to steal the good things that our Father has given to us. Do not let the enemy win against you. Put on the full armor of God (*Ephesians 6:11-13*) and fight back. Keep moving forward despite the troubles that come your way, and one day you will reach your God-given destiny.

Do not let tough times immobilize you. Instead, confront your problems one on one. Do not give in to despair. Keep facing your problems, not running away from them or ignoring them.

If you make excuses for not dealing with your problems, believe me, they will make a home in your life. Instead, fight back with all your might and keep trusting God to make things better for you. Expect Him to fight on your behalf, and you will soon begin to see your situation improving.

God has great things in store for you. Do not settle for less. If God has put a dream in you, do not let go of it just because you have suffered a setback. Keep going, keep believing, and keep trusting God. Expect Him to come through for you, and you will not be disappointed. He is able to do exceedingly, abundantly above all that we can ever ask Him!

Chapter 1

The Power of Your Tongue

It is a reality of life that all of us pass through dark times. Times when all the walls seem to close in on us. Times when every single door seems to shut in our face. Dark times that make us feel all alone. During such times, it is imperative that we speak positive words to bring about a change in our situation.

The Bible shows us clearly how important our words are. There is power in the words that come out of our mouths. *Revelation 12:11* talks of believers who overcame the devil "by the blood of the Lamb, and *by the word of their testimony."* Romans 10:9 assures us that "if you *confess with your mouth* the Lord Jesus and believe in your heart that God has raised Him from the dead, you will be saved."

The truth is that something happens in the spiritual realm every time you utter a word. Your words have creative power. Whatever you say will come to pass—whether it is positive or negative.

But how often do we speak negative words to ourselves or our loved ones? Words like, "I am so broke"; or, "I am not equal to that task because I am not well educated"; or, "I will never get out of debt". Or, better still, we call our children "stupid", "foolish" or "you good-for-nothing, you will never succeed!" How often? Many times.

The truth is that every time we make a negative statement about ourselves or others, we create the very thing we speak out. The enemy takes whatever comes out of our mouths and makes it come to pass. I once read a book by a former Satanist who got born again. He was narrating how he and his friends used to go near the homes of people—especially Christians—and eavesdrop on what they were saying. Every time a born-again Christian said a negative word, they would take that word and make it come to pass.

For example, if you say, "We are so broke" or "Our finances are going down the drain", the devil will steal every dollar from you and make sure that your finances really are going down the drain. Or, when you have a headache and you say, "This headache is killing me," the truth is that the headache just might kill you, if you don't change your way of talking.

The Power of Your Tongue

I know how very difficult it is to stay positive when life is hard. Maybe you don't have food to eat today, or your landlord is threatening to throw you out of his house because you owe him three months' rent. Or your children have dropped out of school because you can't afford to pay their school fees. In life, we often go through dark times that make us wonder whether God really does care about us. We pray and stay in faith, and still nothing happens. But, despite everything that you are going through, it is important that you declare positive words over your situation.

Get up every morning and say, "Even though this is happening to me, I know I am blessed, I have a bright future, and God will meet all my needs according to the riches of His glory in Christ Jesus." The enemy will always try to convince you that your problem is too big to be solved. But do not believe the devil's lies. Instead, keep on affirming that Jehovah Jireh is your Provider and that He is coming to your rescue.

Reject the devil's lies. When he tells you that you cannot make it, open your mouth and say, "I will make it, I am more than a conqueror, I am blessed, I will prosper, and I will succeed even if the situation seems bad now." Boldly declare positive words into your situation. God will take your words of faith and bring to pass in the natural world what you have created in the spiritual world.

It is a sad fact of life that, in our darkest hour when we most need comfort, we often see nothing but doors shutting on us. That is the time when even our closest friends will go against us. The very friend we once helped out of a financial crisis (and now we hope will lend us a hand in return) is the same one who will either completely ignore us or sit in judgment over us, accusing us of bringing it all upon ourselves. But there is someone who will never leave us or forsake us. When you are left all alone and completely heartbroken, that is the time to look up and say, like the Psalmist David:

> I lift up my eyes to the mountains—
>   where does my help come from?
> My help comes from the LORD,
>   the Maker of heaven and earth.
>
> *Psalm 121:1-2, NIV*

After all, your Father is the very same God who created the people you were trying to get help from. Why not go to Him directly? The Bible says that He who watches over you will neither slumber nor sleep (*Psalm 121:3-4*).

The Power of Your Tongue

Tell the devil, "God, who watches over me, is awake. He knows what I am going through, and He will come through for me." Sometimes God allows us to go through tough times so that we can learn to depend on Him totally. These are the times when everyone has turned their back on you, and even your own parents do not want to see you or offer a helping hand. But, when you learn to depend upon the One who created you, your circumstances will always change for the better.

After all, who can best help you, other than the One who created you? He knows every cell in your body; He knew you even before you were formed in your mother's womb (*Psalm 139:13-16*). Before your mother even knew she was carrying you in her womb, God knew you. Imagine that!

He knew you would be born into that family. He knows what you are going through, and He knows exactly how to get you through those difficulties, if only you will put your faith in Him. Keep on blessing your life by speaking positive words. Remind God of His promises. Remind Him of His steadfast love and wait for Him to come through for you.

It does not matter what situation you are in. What matters is—what are you saying about your situation? Are you going to come out of those tough times a better or a bitter person? One who knows how to depend upon God—or one who is full of resentment, always cursing everyone else? I pray that you will come out victorious, to the glory of God the Father.

I remember a time when my finances were at rock bottom and my cousin was getting married. I did not have a dress to wear to the wedding, let alone shoes. I went down on my knees and cried to God to provide for me. At my age, I did not want to ask my mum for money to buy a dress. I told God, "Father, you know my situation. If I do not go to that wedding, people will talk very badly. I do not want to ask anyone for money to buy a dress, so please provide for me. After all, you are my Father." Then I said Amen.

The wedding was drawing really close, and I still didn't have any money. Three days to the wedding, a girl I was staying with found some money someone had dropped on the ground. When she gave me the money and told me how she had found it, the first thing that came to my mind was that it must be from the devil because it was so much money coming from a little girl.

The Power of Your Tongue

We prayed and asked God to take away the money if it had any connection with the devil. We waited, but the money did not disappear. So I went ahead and bought a dress and a pair of shoes and wore them to my cousin's wedding. Indeed, God provides for us if we keep in faith!

All that time I was waiting for something to happen, I had no doubt in my mind that my Father would provide. As much as the devil kept reminding me that the wedding was drawing close and I had nothing to wear, so much more did I keep on saying, "Father, I know you will not disappoint me, I know you will not let me be ashamed." Sure enough, my Father came through for me.

If I had listened to the devil's lies, do you think God would have provided for me? Of course not! He rewards only those who stay in faith. If I had succumbed to despair, I would not have been able to get new clothes. In the natural course of events, I would have gone to the wedding in my old attire, and all my relatives would have noticed I was the only one there in a worn-out dress.

Our God is a loving God, and He is more than willing to bless you. He wants you to live in plenty, be successful, marry a godly spouse, and have a happy home. The enemy on the other hand knows that we have a loving Father who is willing and ready to give us anything and everything. That is why Satan keeps on bringing bad things our way.

The Bible says, "Many are the afflictions of the righteous, but the LORD delivers him out of them all." (*Psalm 34:19*) Now note this: the Lord delivers us, not out of *some* of these afflictions, but out of ***all*** of them. So, learn to put your trust and faith in God. Speak words of faith every minute you get, and God will come through for you!

Four months after I gave birth to my son Ryan, my husband—who worked as a policeman—had to go on an assignment with other police officers to a remote part of our country. Their mission was to recover some cattle that had been stolen from one community by a rival community. That meant my husband, whom I loved very much, had to leave us at my mother's house. My son and I tearfully bade him "Goodbye", and he left.

The journey took them two days. The area was so remote that phone signals were almost nil. After a week, the policemen received intelligence on where to find the cattle. They set out for the place at night, intending to take the enemy by surprise. But the cattle rustlers got wind of their plan and maneuvered themselves so well that no policeman could have escaped alive. Remember that they knew the terrain much better than the policemen.

A fierce battle broke out between the policemen and the cattle rustlers. Back home, my spirit told me something was wrong. I kept calling my husband, but his phone was switched off. Hours passed while I kept on calling and not reaching him. It was habitual for him to call me every morning and evening; so when mid-day came and I had still not received any call from him, I knew something was definitely wrong.

At six o'clock, I called the wife of another policeman who had also gone on the mission. I got a shock when she said her husband had called and told her the situation was bad and some policemen had been wounded. Right that minute I told God, "Please bring my husband back home to me."

I covered my husband with the blood of Jesus, declaring that he would live and not die. I told the devil that he was a liar and that my family was covered by the blood of Jesus. In tears, I saw on TV that 15 policemen had been killed and scores injured. I felt a cloud of darkness surrounding me, but I told God, "As surely as you are alive, I will not lose faith. My husband will come back to me."

It's Not Over Yet

I called my husband once, but I could not reach him. So many thoughts raced through my mind. The devil kept telling me that my husband was dead and that I would be called to go and identify his body... and what would I tell our son? How would I tell him about a father he would never know? But I pushed back all those thoughts and shouted, "My husband is not dead!"

Then my husband called me. He said that he had been wounded but, apart from that, he was alright. When he came home, he narrated to me how God had miraculously saved him on the battlefield. The first bullet from the enemy was aimed at his head, but it did not kill him. While the rest of the policemen managed to get under cover, he could not find any place to hide from the enemy. But, despite being exposed to the cattle rustlers, they could not kill him. God protected him. He watched his colleagues die, while he survived. I was so humbled by the faithfulness of our God.

God asked Moses, "What is that in your hand?"

"A staff," Moses replied. And God told him to throw it down on the ground. (*Exodus 4:2-3*)

At that moment of crisis, I was totally helpless. I did not know what to do, but I knew I had to give God something to work with—my words spoken positively. I had nothing in my hand but my words—but they were enough for God to work His miracle for me.

I do not know what situation you are in right now—maybe even tougher than the one I had gone through. What you say at that defining moment will determine what God will do for you—or what your enemy will do against you.

The Bible says that those who trust in the Lord will never be put to shame (*1 Peter 2:6*). Our words spoken in faith will avail much, for God is pleased with a person who stays in faith. Just as God "gives life to the dead and calls those things which do not exist as though they did" (*Romans 4:17*), in the same way, start speaking of things which do not exist (but you wish they did) as though they did; start speaking life into lifeless situations. That is faith!

God tells us that, without faith, it is impossible to please Him (*Hebrews 11:6*). So why not create your own specific answer to your prayer by speaking to your situation and letting God answer you? Because He surely will. The Bible says that "every *tongue* should *confess* that Jesus Christ is Lord" (*Philippians 2:11*). Note that it does not say every mind should think that Jesus Christ is Lord. God created our tongues for a reason—for us to use them to speak life into our lifeless situations, to command blessings into our lives, to reject every bad thing that comes our way.

It does not matter how you feel. You can be feeling terrible because of what you are going through. What matters are your words spoken in faith. God has put inside each of us the key to life and death. That key is your tongue. It is squarely within your control. It is entirely up to you to use the God-given power of your tongue to bless your life and the lives of those around you. You can create a good future for yourself and your children through your words.

This was what happened to my friend James. Born to a single mother, he grew up very poor, and his mother had to struggle hard to put him through school. James did well in high school and was accepted into the university. I remember him telling me, "You know, one day I will be a rich man."

Considering that he was living in a mud house at the time and barely had three square meals a day, I thought, "Wow, my friend, you have to win the lottery to get yourself out of this mess and have enough to live on; then you can be counted as rich."

The Power of Your Tongue

After graduating from university, he could not get a job, so he decided to start his own small business. He told me he had 10,000 shillings in his bank account and he was determined to open a shop. He rented a shop space for 2,000 shillings a month, paying the money upfront. He used up the remaining 8,000 shillings in his account to buy goods and pay for transporting them to his shop.

James spoke life into his business. As the days went by, his shop grew so big that he became the wholesale supplier to the other shops around him. Today he is a rich man. He no longer lives in a mud house because he has built himself a beautiful home. He has also bought land for his mother and built her a house.

What does this teach us? That we should watch what comes out of our mouths! James could have just sat back and moaned, "My mother isn't able to provide well for me, so I am doomed to fail." But he decided to create his own destiny with his words. It is up to you to determine your own future, because what you say is what you will get.

When you speak words of faith, God has already agreed with you. He tells us that, if we ask anything of Him, He will do it for us (*John 14:14*). I used to ask myself—why do we still need to ask for anything when He already knows everything we need? Then understanding came to me: He wants us to open our mouths and tell Him what we want. After all, we are His children. I don't know about you but, if my children ask me for anything, I will gladly give it to them (if I am able to). Let us make full use of our privileges as children of the Most High God and tell Him what we want.

There was this lady who planted potatoes on her farm. She had invested so much in the farm. Then the worst happened: it rained so hard, much more than was usual, and frost set in. Generally, potatoes do not like frost. They normally freeze to death. This lady, having used up all her money to lease the land and invest in her crop of potatoes, had no money left to buy frost protectors to prevent her potatoes from freezing. But she knew who she was—the child of the Most High God.

She went around her farm, speaking to the potatoes and frost. I can imagine her saying, "Frost, these are my farm's boundaries and these are my potato plants. You are not going to touch any of those potatoes!" She went around the farm over and over again, repeating the same words to the frost and potatoes. Then she went home, convinced that the potatoes and the frost had heard her.

The Power of Your Tongue

That night, nature unleashed her full fury and snow fell like never before. Amazingly, it never touched this lady's farm. Not a single potato was touched by the frost. All the other farms around suffered heavy damage from the frost but not hers. She later harvested a plentiful crop of potatoes—all because of the power of her words. She understood who she was and the power that was in her words.

In times of trouble, start commanding your situation to change. Don't let the enemy preach to you the gospel of defeat and failure: that you are doomed to fail, that things must get worse before they get better. These are the devil's lies; refute them and put the devil in his place. Bless your life, and it will surely be blessed.

Can you imagine how victorious you will be, once you learn to speak words of faith into your life? Our Father loves us with an everlasting love. He says that He has inscribed us on the palms of His hands (*Isaiah 49:16*) and we are the apple of His eye (*Zechariah 2:8*). This means that, when we get hurt, He feels it first.

If something got into your eye, would you just leave it there? Or would you make every effort to remove it? Definitely, you would have it removed! How closely knit is He to us, that when we hurt, He hurts as well! And, when we are happy, He is happy as well! We are indeed loved.

Today, make a choice to speak positive, constructive words into your life. God created us to enjoy life, to live abundant lives, to be more than conquerors (*Romans 8:37*), and not to live defeated, mediocre lives. Remember that God has put the power of life and death in your tongue.

Only you have the key to what you want to be, to where you want to go, to what you want your children to be. That key is your tongue; it has the power to bless or curse. Go ahead and use it constructively, and see how your situation will turn around for you.

Chapter 2

Remember Past Victories

God did not create us to live a life of defeat but to overcome the challenges we face. The enemy, on the other hand, wants us to give up and believe that God does not love us, and that is why He is letting us suffer so much. Do not be deceived by the devil's lies.

Stop focusing on your problems, and focus instead on what God has done for you in the past. Remember how many times you have been sick and cried to God; how He heard you and healed you. Remember how God has protected you from diseases that were taking peoples' lives by the minute; how He has been protecting you from those road accidents that have claimed thousands of lives—yet you are alive today!

It is imperative that you realize this: *the same God who has given you so many victories in the past has not changed.* He is still faithful. He is waiting for you to trust Him. Have faith in Him, no matter how bad the circumstances may seem. Trust Him to turn that financial lack into abundance, that failing marriage into a happy one, that sickness into good health. Have an expectant mind; wake up every day expecting God to do a new thing in your life, to solve that problem and to put a new song in your heart.

I remember when my husband and I were trying to have a baby. We had to wait five months before I could conceive. When I did get pregnant, I started developing problems almost immediately. At that time, we were living in a rented apartment, and we had a neighbor who claimed to be a gynecologist. He offered to help us—at a cost, of course! He said I had to be injected every week with some boosters to help retain the pregnancy.

Week after week I got the injections, but I felt something was wrong. I started doubting the "doctor", but I didn't dare to stop the medications as I wanted the baby. My intuition refused to leave me alone, and I continued to feel that something was terribly wrong. But when I told the "doctor", he said I should be strong and there was nothing wrong. He told me not to consult any other doctor because he was the only one who knew what he had given me. After twelve weeks, I lost my baby.

Remember Past Victories

My husband and I were devastated, but we had one consolation—I did not die. I was still alive; that meant I had another chance to have a baby. I was very angry with that "doctor"—especially after we asked around and found out he wasn't a qualified doctor at all, but a quack.

When we asked him what drugs he had given me, so that I could be sure to avoid them and not ruin my chances of having a baby again, he categorically refused to tell me. In fact, he told me to my face, "Naomy, you will look for me to help you so that you can be pregnant again! Otherwise, you will never have a child with your husband."

I felt like pouncing on him and practically throttling the life out of him; but I didn't. I looked him in the eye and said, "You are not God—and, as long as God is alive, I will get pregnant!"

I remembered how God had helped me to conceive that first time. It had taken me five months of tears before I became pregnant. I knew in my heart that it was God who had done it for me. That was why, even after I had lost the baby and despite my fear that maybe that quack doctor had interfered with my hormones, I continued to put my trust in God my Creator. I believed that He would give me another baby.

It's Not Over Yet

I said to Him, "You are the Giver of life. Give me a child so that that quack can see your power." And God did it again. Two months later, I became pregnant, and eventually I gave birth to a healthy baby boy. Now, what if I had listened to that quack of a doctor? What if I had believed what he said, that I would never be able to have a baby? The devil would have won!

What problem are you facing that seems so big it makes you think God has forsaken you? Do not let those thoughts take root inside of you. God can never forget you, if you stay in faith and in prayer. He is our loving Father, and He has given you more than enough ammunition to win your battles. Remember the times He has come through for you in the past? He will do it again, if you will let Him. Stay focused on the greatness of our God, not on the size of your problem.

God is for you and not against you. The Bible tells us that He thinks good thoughts about us, thoughts to give us a future and a hope—that doesn't sound like a God who has forgotten you!

> For I know the thoughts that I think toward you, says the LORD, thoughts of peace and not of evil, to give you a future and a hope.
>
> *Jeremiah 29:11*

Remember Past Victories

Remember Shadrach, Meshach and Abednego? They refused to bow down and worship the king's idol, even if it meant that they would have to die a terrible death (*Daniel 3:1-23*). I can imagine the tremendous pressure they were under, the perilous situation they were in. It was them against the whole country—thousands of people bowing before the golden statue; but not those three.

Why didn't they worship the idol? Because they knew that the One they believed in would be more than able to help them in their darkest hour. They never lost their faith in God. They remembered the many times the God of Israel had rescued them in their own country and how He had favored them, even in that foreign land of Babylon to which they had been brought by their captors. They had no doubt that, what God did in the past, He was more than able to do over and over again. That was why they had the courage to tell the king:

> "Our God whom we serve is able to deliver us from the burning fiery furnace, and He will deliver us from your hand, O king. But if not, let it be known to you, O king, that we do not serve your gods, nor will we worship the gold image which you have set up."
>
> *Daniel 3:17-18*

It's Not Over Yet

I don't think your situation can be any worse than theirs. Notice how they kept their cool and honored God in the process... and how God honored them in return! What an awesome experience it must have been, to be walking unharmed in the fiery furnace with the King of kings!

> Then King Nebuchadnezzar was astonished; and he rose in haste and spoke, saying to his counselors, "Did we not cast three men bound into the midst of the fire?"
> They answered and said to the king, "True, O king."
> "Look!" he answered, "I see four men loose, walking in the midst of the fire; and they are not hurt, and the form of the fourth is like the Son of God."
>
> *Daniel 3:24-25*

When you are at the bottom of the valley, broken and not knowing what to do next, that is when the enemy closes in for the kill—telling you how you will never rise again; how your marriage is going up in smoke; how your finances are going down the drain; how your health has deteriorated and you are at death's door. Do not listen to him; he is a liar and the father of lies (*John 8:44, NIV*).

Remember Past Victories

Think of the many testimonies you have heard from God's children, praising and thanking their Creator for coming through for them. Claim your own victory as well. If He could do it for them, I do not see anything different with you. He can and will do it for you.

Open your mouth and declare, "I thank you, Lord, for the many miracles you have done in your children's lives. I believe you are able to get me out of this situation because I too am your child." Remind Him of His promises to His people and His everlasting faithfulness. He will surely outdo Himself.

Habakkuk must have been at the bottom of the valley when he said, "Lord, I have heard of your fame; I stand in awe of your deeds, Lord. Repeat them in our day." (*Habakkuk 3:2a, NIV*) He went on to say, "In this time of our deep need, begin again to help us, as you did in years gone by. Show us your power to save us." (*Habakkuk 3:2b, TLB*)

He went on to remind God of the great things He had done for His people; how He had delivered them out of Egypt and took them through the Red Sea. For forty years, God provided for them and protected them in every way. Habakkuk asked God to do the same for His people in his day.

It's Not Over Yet

What about the children of Israel, when they got to the Red Sea? God had fought for them in Egypt and forced Pharaoh to let them go; but, after such a mighty victory, they arrived at the Red Sea—and there was no way to get across. Hot on their heels was Pharaoh's great army, ready to take them captive or kill them. Some of the Israelites gave in to despair, but one man remembered the past victories God had wrought for them.

Moses told them, "These men you are seeing today, you will never see again." He lifted his staff; the sea opened and made way for the Israelites. When all of them had crossed the sea, he bought down his staff, and the waters flowed back and drowned Pharaoh's entire army. (*Exodus 14:21-28*)

Learn to trust God, even in your darkest hour. Even when it is humanly impossible to do so. That is why we are a peculiar people; we laugh when we should be crying. We laugh because we have a God who fights for us and gives us the victory.

> But ye are a chosen generation, a royal priesthood, an holy nation, a peculiar people; that ye should shew forth the praises of him who hath called you out of darkness into his marvelous light.
>
> *1 Peter 2:9, KJV*

Remember Past Victories

When you are facing tough times, it does not mean God has forgotten you. Sometimes, we have to go through trials so that we can grow spiritually. When you accepted Jesus as your Lord and Savior, He did not promise you a life free of problems or hardships. But He did promise that He would never leave you or forsake you (*Hebrews 13:5*).

Do not listen to naysayers—those people who are always telling you that you will never get well, never get out of debt, or that your marriage is a failure, your life is a failure, and so on and so forth. No! Remember that no one has any right to write the ending to your story. The only one who has the final word is God Himself; and, if you stay in faith, He will help you and guide you out of all your problems.

Do not let your troubles take you away from God. Constantly thinking about them will wear you down, leaving you with little energy to pray. Instead, turn your thoughts towards the goodness of God, and make every effort to pray to Him in your darkest moments.

Tell Him, "Father, I thank you that, though I feel so weak, your strength is made perfect in my weakness. Come and be my strength and help me stay in faith. I am putting my trust in you alone."

It's Not Over Yet

Take a step of faith and, slowly but surely, God will enable you to pray amidst all that you are going through. You may be tempted to say, "But I am so sick and I feel like my time has come. I might not come out of this one." But let me remind you that, despite your illness, you are alive today. You are not dead yet, and you can even read this book.

Can you imagine how many people went to bed last night and never woke up this morning? God has given you this gift of today. Every day is a gift from God. The fact that you are still breathing means that you have a chance to better yourself, to stay in faith, to claim your healing, to claim blessings for yourself and your family, to tell others about the goodness of God. Life has given you a chance to do something good.

When you wake up in the morning, make a deliberate choice to declare victory over your circumstances. Remember, it is not over unless you let it be. I heard a testimony recently from a young man who had contracted HIV. In spite of visiting doctor after doctor, his health was failing fast. In fact, he was wasting away so badly that, at the age of 30, he weighed only 25kg. He had grown so skinny and weak that he was just skin and bones, and he had sores all over his body.

Remember Past Victories

Though he was on ARVs, they were not helping him much. One day he heard a servant of the Lord on the radio, praying for the sick. After the prayer, people began to call in with their testimonies. One testimony in particular caught his attention: it was from a brother in Christ, telling listeners how God had miraculously healed him of AIDS.

This young man began to claim his healing from that point onwards. He told God, "If you did it for him, you can do it for me as well." After saying that simple prayer, he felt stronger. In fact, he felt so much better that his pastor offered to take him to a doctor, to find out if he had really been healed. At the clinic, they asked the doctor to test him again for HIV. The doctor was confused at first, as the young man had been his patient for some time; but he acceded to their request.

The results showed he did not have the virus. Shocked, the doctor told them he would have to repeat the tests, this time with advanced machines. They were asked to return to the clinic the next day for the test results, which they did. This second set of results confirmed that he was HIV-free.

The doctor could not understand what was happening. The young man narrated how he had been healed by God after listening to the testimony on the radio. The doctor told him to return three months later for another test.

It's Not Over Yet

After the three months had gone by, he was sent to a hospital, this time to test for HIV DNA. I have been told this is the final test that will confirm for sure whether one is free of the virus or not. He took the test and it came out negative as well. Today this young man is healthy and HIV-free, and he is preaching the gospel of our Lord Jesus.

Whatever you are struggling with today, there are other people who have faced the same problem, and God has come through for them. It may not be an illness; it may be an addiction to alcohol, a marriage gone wrong, or a financial difficulty, or maybe you have lost your job. Remind yourself that God has delivered His children out of all their troubles, and claim the same help for yourself.

Who says your situation is any worse than what others have gone through? Our God is bigger than any problem. What He has done for others, He is well able to do for you. Every victory against the enemy builds your faith in God and in His power. It makes you realize He is real, He listens to your prayers, and He keeps His promises to us. God is true to His Word. When He says He will always be there for us, He means every single word.

You may be saying, "But God has never done any miracle for me to remember." Friend, that is not

Remember Past Victories

true. He may not have healed you, or given you a promotion at your workplace, or handed you a fortune. But the fact that you are alive today is miracle enough to give thanks to God. The fact that you are healthy—although you may not have a job—is reason enough for you to thank God and to believe that the right job is on the way.

There is something that God has done for each one of us at one time or another. Keep counting your blessings; keep counting what you have, not what you do not have. Instead of complaining that you did not get that promotion you thought you deserved and it was given to someone else, thank Him that at least you have a job.

Keep thanking Him for the small things that people take for granted. Thank Him that you were born whole. Can you imagine how many people are physically challenged? Keep trusting in Him to do great things in your life.

If you stay thankful, constantly reminding yourself that you are alive by God's grace, you will have peace in your heart. You will be happier, and you will have the assurance that God will come through for you.

Chapter 3

Do Not Listen to Negative Voices

Negative voices are often heard the loudest when we least need them. Those times when we are facing the toughest challenges of our lives, that is when even the people closest to us tend to make negative comments that leave us feeling even more discouraged than we already are.

They will keep telling you that, hey, you still have that financial problem which is not going to go away any time soon; so stop thinking about how you can go on a holiday, or how you can buy a new house, because it isn't going to happen. Or maybe they will remind you that you are sick and the doctor says you only have a few months to live, and therefore you should not make any future plans. Or, how about this—just leave your spouse, he (or she) doesn't deserve you?

The truth is, the people closest to us are the ones who think they know us better than we know ourselves. Some even believe they should plan our lives for us because, according to them, they know

DO NOT LISTEN TO NEGATIVE VOICES

all there is to know about us, and more. But is that always the case? Do you really think your friends know you so well that they can make decisions on your behalf; and you will have to go along with them? I doubt it.

As much as these friends love you and want the best for you, you are the only one who knows what you want. When you are taking the hard knocks of life, the one feeling the pain is you. You are the only one who knows where the shoe hurts most. The determining factor here is not anyone else; it is you! You are the only person who knows what you want for yourself and your family. Do not listen to negative people who will only hurt and not help you.

Always be careful because, when you are at the lowest point of your life, that's when the devil will use people close to you to plant seeds of doubt, discouragement and despair in your life. Once these seeds take root, destruction will surely come; you will not be able to get of your predicament.

Remember the power of words. Words create; and if you let negative words get through to your mind and take root in your heart, they will create negative outcomes in your life. Cancel every negative word with a positive one. Tell yourself:

you are down, but not out; you may be out of a job, but that doesn't mean you will never get another job; you are sick, but that doesn't mean you will not get well; your marriage is shaky, but that doesn't mean it won't stabilize; it's not the end of you.

You need to surround yourself with people who will stand by you in faith and encourage you to attain your dreams. Avoid those who constantly bring you down when you are already feeling weak.

When our Lord Jesus was about to be crucified on the cross, it was the darkest hour of His human life. He knew how painful it would be, to have those huge nails go through His wrists and feet. He was afraid; but He knew He had to go through all that suffering to save us.

Peter tried to talk Him out of going to the cross. Jesus realized that, if He went on listening to this well-meaning disciple, it would weaken His resolve to die on the cross for us—which was the very reason He came to earth. Though Peter was close to Him, Jesus had to rebuke the devil in him. "Get behind Me, Satan!" He said (*Mark 8:33*).

Now, note that this was the very same disciple Jesus took with Him everywhere He went. The devil often uses people we trust and love to try to dissuade us from fulfilling our destiny, just as he tried to do with Jesus.

Do Not Listen to Negative Voices

The funny thing about friends is that, more often than not, they will try to talk you out of your blessings. Don't allow that to happen to you.

How many times have you wanted to do something to better your life, only to have a close friend or a relative talk you out of it? Telling you how impossible it would be to achieve your goal? Making you doubt your ability to make it—yet, deep down in your heart, you had this conviction that you could have succeeded? Many times, I am sure. Or at least it happened at one time or another.

Don't get me wrong, I am not saying you should live like a recluse and keep away from your family and friends—No! I am only saying that you should be careful what gets into your head. Choose only advice that is helpful to you, and disregard the rest.

When Moses sent twelve people out to spy out the Promised Land, they came back with an excellent report. They said that the land was fertile and beautiful. But ten of them had a very negative report as well; they said it was impossible to take the land because of the giants living in it.

Joshua and Caleb, however, believed otherwise. They assured the people that, though the giants were indeed formidable, God would help them take the land, as He had promised to their forefathers. (*Numbers 14:6-9*)

It's Not Over Yet

No doubt, the problem was a humongous one. And, no doubt, the inhabitants of the land were way bigger than the Israelites. With all due respect, any human being would have been shaken. But not Joshua and Caleb. They looked back and saw how God had rescued them from the Egyptians and fought great battles for them. They were convinced that He was able to help them overcome the giants and take the land that was rightfully theirs.

When you are facing gigantic problems, you need to surround yourself with men and women of faith. Listen to people who will strengthen your faith and help you reach your destiny. Do not listen to those who will hinder you from getting what God has in store for you.

When you are down, God knows a way out. The very fact that you are in this seemingly impossible situation means that God knows you have what it takes to get out of the situation; otherwise He would not have allowed that situation to come your way.

When you are at your lowest, that is the time to hone your skills in fighting the battle of faith. The Bible says that without faith it is impossible to please God (*Hebrews 11:6*) and that faith comes by hearing the word of God (*Romans 10:17*). What you hear is important; it is imperative to understand that what you allow into your ears will take root in your heart and decide the course of your life.

Do Not Listen to Negative Voices

The ten men who gave a bad report never got to the Promised Land. God swore they would die in the wilderness, together with all those who had believed their negative words. Why? Because they did not believe that God would fight for them against their enemies and take the land for them.

Imagine that! The only mistake that led to a whole generation of Israelites not getting to the Promised Land but dying in the wilderness was that they listened to a negative report delivered by their own people. People will hinder you from receiving what God wants to give you, if you allow their negative voices to influence you.

Why would you want to die in poverty simply because you have been talked into believing that God will not provide for you? Why let your marriage go down the drain because a friend told you it couldn't work and you are "not the marrying type"? Why die, simply because your doctor told you that you had an incurable illness? Do you not have a God who is Jehovah Rapha your Healer?

Recently, I was watching a movie that exposed the ugly side of human nature. It was about two brothers: a very wealthy man and his younger, poverty-stricken sibling. The young man went to his rich brother to ask for money to start a business.

It's Not Over Yet

He told his brother that he wanted to set up a shop selling certain kinds of goods to the people in his hometown. He had found out that there was a great demand for those goods, but no one was supplying them to the people in the area.

The elder brother knew the idea was a brilliant one and would make the young man a great deal of money. But he refused to help, saying that he was short of cash. This of course was just an excuse; he simply did not want his brother to get ahead in life!

He went so far as to lie to the poor man that it would be impossible to import those kinds of goods and he would need a large sum of money to buy them from overseas suppliers. He even made up a story about how a friend of his had started the same kind of business and failed miserably. Discouraged, the younger brother went back home, not knowing what to do next.

In reality, the rich brother wanted to maintain the status quo. He wanted to make sure that he was the only one who was well off and that his younger brother would have to keep going to him to beg for handouts. Often, the people who discourage you from following your dreams actually want you to remain where you are in life.

Do Not Listen to Negative Voices

Blind Bartimaeus sat begging by the roadside. When he heard that the Lord Jesus was passing by, he said to himself, "I have heard of the many miracles He has performed, and I have no doubt in my mind that, if I could meet face to face with Him, my life will never be the same again."

He started shouting, "Jesus, Son of David, have mercy on me!" The people around him told him to shut up. But he cried out all the more, "Son of David, have mercy on me!" I like his persistence.

Jesus stopped and asked him, "What do you want Me to do for you?"

Bartimaeus replied, "I want to see."

Then Jesus said to him, "Go your way; your faith has made you well." And immediately he received his sight. (*Mark 10:52*)

Didn't Jesus know that Bartimaeus was there and needed help? Of course He knew! But He was waiting for the blind man to take a step of faith and ask Him for help. He was waiting for him to block his ears to the many people telling him to shut up.

What if Bartimaeus had listened to those negative voices and given up? What if he had not cried out to the Lord? That miracle could have passed him by—while, in reality, it was meant for him from the very beginning. The people telling him to shut up were used to seeing him begging on the streets for a few coins, and they wanted him to remain the same. Perhaps it gave them a sense of superiority over him.

The best thing that can happen to you when you are going through tough times is to get fed up with your situation. Do not resign yourself to your "fate"; do not let apathy set in. When we are facing challenges, we tend after a while to lose hope that we can ever overcome them. We begin to accept that those problems are here to stay. We convince ourselves that we have to learn to live with them.

Of course some situations are permanent, like the death of a loved one. But, more often than not, there is a way out. If you are alive today, you have an opportunity to change your financial situation. You can still do something about that addiction, that broken relationship. Where there is life, there is always a chance to better your life.

Speak life to that problem. Do not settle for less, go for the best. It does not matter how hopeless the situation looks, there is hope as long as you are still breathing. All you have to do is to get fed up enough to take action.

Sometimes we are our own worst enemy; we allow negative thoughts to cloud our minds. When we do that, those thoughts take root in our minds.

Do Not Listen to Negative Voices

We need to stop telling ourselves, "I am so poor, if I just have a little food to eat today, I won't ask for more." Or, "This illness has taken a toll on my health, but I'll just have to learn to live with it."

If you accept the problem as being part of you, it will not go away! After all, it has found a home in you, as long as you keep on being negative. And, when you keep on replaying negative thoughts in your mind, you are fertilizing the ground for that problem to take root in your life; you are constantly watering it so that it grows even bigger and eventually bears fruit!

You have to start changing your mindset. Say something positive; tell yourself, "I am blessed, my Father owns the universe, I am prosperous, I am a conqueror, and my best days are still ahead of me. I will be whole; this sickness is not here to stay. This is a passing cloud in my life."

My cousin and his wife were still childless after ten years of marriage. His parents tried to get him to leave his wife because she could not give him a child, but he loved her too much to give in to their demands. Year after year, they prayed for a child, but nothing happened. I remember my cousin's wife telling me how her sister-in-law would constantly insult her, saying that she would never become a mother. But, despite those words hurting her very deeply, she did not let them take root. She believed that one day God would give her a child.

It's Not Over Yet

The problem grew so bad that they became the talk of the whole village. My cousin's father would not allow them to build a house on his farm, so they had to rent one elsewhere. In fact, they were treated as outcasts by their own family members. But eventually God came through for them and, after ten years, they are now proud parents of a beautiful baby girl.

If my cousin had listened to all the people who advised him to end his marriage, the devil would have won. Do not fall into the enemy's trap by listening to negative voices; remember that Satan comes to steal, kill and destroy (*John 10:10*).

The worst part is that, after you have followed the bad advice, the very same people who gave it to you will be laughing at you. Can you imagine what would have happened if my cousin had taken their advice and ended his marriage? People would be talking about how he sent his wife packing simply because she could not give him a child!

The same people who used to say my cousin will never have a child now have no choice but to acknowledge that God is alive and able to answer the prayers of His children. Every testimony that comes out of a difficult situation always glorifies and honors God our Father.

Do Not Listen to Negative Voices

When I look at that child, my heart is filled with praises to God for the way He came through for my cousin and his wife. The whole village now has a new song—a song of praise and worship to God. That makes the devil a defeated, frustrated and humiliated enemy, just the way it should be.

Friend, do not accept what you are going through as a death sentence. What God has done for others, He is well able to do for you. He wants you to have a wonderful life filled with His blessings, abundance and good health. He says that if we stay in faith, no good thing will He withhold from us (*Psalm 84:11*). Indeed, He is faithful.

Public opinion is the greatest destroyer of destiny. When you allow people to run your life, it will hinder you from becoming all that God created you to be. It will keep you from getting all that God intended you to have. Those discouraging voices are helping the devil to build a stronghold in your life. Learn to block them out, the way Jesus did.

"My little daughter lies at the point of death. Come and lay Your hands on her, that she may be healed, and she will live," Jairus begged Jesus (*Mark 5:23*). He knew for sure that if he could get Jesus to pray for his child, she would be well again.

It's Not Over Yet

Just then some people came and told him not to disturb Jesus as his daughter had already died. But Jesus assured him, "Do not be afraid; only believe." In other words, Jesus was telling him, "I am the Way, the Truth and the Life; just believe in Me, and everything will be fine!"

I can imagine how Jairus must have held on to those words, "Do not be afraid." When you have the Lord Jesus by your side, nothing should shake you, not even death.

When Jesus reached the house, everyone there was weeping and wailing. He asked, "Why make this commotion and weep? The child is not dead, but sleeping." And they ridiculed Him.

So what did Jesus do? The Bible reports that He "put them all outside"—everyone except the child's parents and His disciples (*Mark 5:39-40*). In other words, He blocked out the negative voices. Then He took the dead girl by the hand, and said to her, "Little girl, I say to you, arise" (*Mark 5:41*). Immediately, she got up and started walking. All those people who had told Jairus not to disturb the Lord or who had laughed at Jesus must have bowed down to worship and give thanks to God for the miracle they had seen with their own eyes.

Do Not Listen to Negative Voices

God has given us everything we need to defeat the enemy. He has given us power over Satan. But every time you allow the devil's lies to get the better of you, every time you listen to people who are being used as his mouthpiece, you are giving the devil ammunition to use against you, to weaken you. You have to fight back.

Nothing ever comes easy; life is a battlefield. We have to fight every single day in order to reach our destiny. You have no choice but to keep fighting because the enemy is in hot pursuit after you. All you have to do is fight back, and the best part is that you and God make the majority in this battle. When you stay in faith and do what God wants you to do, you will win the battle of life.

I have never heard of an army that fights against itself. When you listen to negative voices and let them influence you in your decisions, you are actually allowing the devil to oppress you even more. Close your ears to those who would tear you down. Believe only what the Holy Spirit tells you, that you are on God's winning side and victory is inevitable. God wants us to enjoy life: to have the best in life, to be in good health, to enjoy our marriage, to excel in business.

It's Not Over Yet

The enemy on the other hand wants to steal all your joy and destroy every good thing in your life, so that you will become bitter and think that God has been unfair to you. He wants to turn you away from God, so that you will miss all of God's blessings.

Do not let yourself stagnate for fear of what people will think or say about you. Move forward and take positive steps to change your situation. Trust in God and believe that He will make all things possible for you.

Chapter 4

Sing Praises to God

In the darkest of hours, nothing seems to work. Nobody seems to understand what you are going through. It's as if there's nothing else left to do other than accept that you are done for. Like nothing will ever be right again. Like everyone has left you to die. Like God doesn't even care at all.

That is the moment the enemy has been waiting for; that is when he starts to celebrate, gloating over your misery, laughing derisively because he has you exactly where he wants you to be.

Friend, do not give up! God has not given up on you. He still wants to work through you. He still wants to show His power through you, even in that dire situation. He still wants to bless you; He still wants to heal you.

When it seems like you have nothing left; when the job you were depending on is no more, because your boss thinks you are no longer useful; when your partner thinks you are no longer important and walks out on you; that is the time to lift your eyes to your Maker and just sing a song of praise.

Yes, it sounds crazy, and you may be asking, "Where will I get the strength to sing when I am feeling at my lowest?" or "How can I even begin to praise Him, when He has allowed this bad thing to happen to me?" But know this: God has allowed it to happen because He knows that you are more than able to overcome the problem.

Praise is a form of worship that God delights in; something supernatural happens when you sing praises to Him. When Paul and Silas were arrested, beaten and thrown into jail for preaching the gospel of our Lord Jesus, they did not hold a pity party there in the prison. They did not start feeling sorry for themselves. Instead, they realized that God had put them there for a reason. They knew that, even if the enemy fought day and night to stop them from spreading the gospel, the will of God would prevail in their lives.

That was why, even in that dungeon, so dark and hopeless, they could sing and praise God. They knew that their God was able to deliver them. The Bible says that, while they were singing praises to God, suddenly there was a great earthquake that shook the prison to its very foundations, and immediately the doors opened and everyone's chains were loosened (*Acts 16:22-25*).

Sing Praises to God

Make a habit of praising God in all situations. If you can praise Him when you are on top of the world, why not do the same when you are at your lowest? The God of the mountaintop is the God of the valley too. The God who gave you that new job, that promotion you didn't expect, that child you wanted: He is with you too, when you have lost your job, when nothing seems to be going right, when someone else got that promotion you thought should be yours because you worked so hard for the company. He has not changed. Why not praise Him the same way you would when things go your way?

Brother Immanuel, a born-again Christian who was once a devil worshipper, revealed how he and his fellow Satanists made life miserable for God's children by invoking curses on them. They would cast spells to inflict poverty and diseases on them, cause their marriages to break up, and destroy relationships between parents and their children.

Once, he was sent on a mission to kill a particular pastor who was making it hard for them to carry out their evil operations. When he got to where the pastor was, he used his occult powers to make an oncoming vehicle lose control so that it would crash into the pastor and kill him.

It's Not Over Yet

The vehicle did lose control and, yes, many people were killed. But, to his amazement, the pastor was not hurt at all. He burst into songs of praise to God, just when the vehicle was about to run him over, and what happened after that took Immanuel's breath away.

Unknown to the pastor, an angel appeared to save him when he started praising God. That was how he so narrowly escaped death. All this happened without the pastor seeing what was going on in the spiritual realm. But Immanuel saw it all.

Friend, great things happen in the spiritual realm when we praise our God. Do not focus on the size of your problem; focus instead on the greatness of our God. Why not thank Him in advance for the things He is going to do for you? Praise and thank Him, and watch Him rescue you. The Bible tells us, "Take your stand [be firm and confident and undismayed] and see the salvation of the Lord which He will accomplish for you today." (*Exodus 14:13, AMP*)

At that defining moment when you are down and out, that is the best time to sing songs of praise to God. Ask Him for His grace to enable you to praise Him in the midst of your problems.

Sing Praises to God

Remember Job? He had everything—immense wealth, beautiful children, a high standing among his peers. But nothing was more important to him than God; he loved God with all his heart. This made Satan jealous, and he accused Job of honoring God only because God had blessed him so greatly. He challenged God to put Job to the test: "But now, stretch out Your hand and touch all that he has, and he will surely curse You to Your face!" (*Job 1:11*)

God took up the challenge because He knew that Job's love for Him was not based on anything He had given him. That was why He gave the devil permission to touch Job's earthly belongings. Job lost everything in a very short time—all his riches and all his children.

How did Job react to this sudden loss of everything he had? The Bible tells us that he fell to the ground and worshipped God. And he said, "The LORD gave, and the LORD has taken away; blessed be the name of the LORD." (*Job 1:20-21*)

Wow! What a man! Instead of whining or complaining about his terrible circumstances, he praised God! It is no wonder, then, that after Job had gone through his season of trial, God gave him twice as much as he had before (*Job 42:10*).

It's Not Over Yet

Praise is a weapon given to us by God Himself. Take time to simply praise Him, and you won't be sorry you did. Thank God in advance for the great miracles He is going to perform in your life. Even when your world is falling apart, just continue to bless the name of the Lord. God will not let His name be put to shame. He will get you out of your situation for His name's sake.

Praise and thank God, not only when you have been blessed with a good job, great relationships and a beautiful home, but also when you are left with nothing. It pleases God when you worship Him at all times; and in return He will manifest Himself in ways you cannot even begin to imagine.

Bob, a gospel artiste, was visiting a lady with breast cancer one day. The cancer had spread so much, it seemed there was no hope left. Not knowing what else to do, they started singing songs of praise to God and blessing Him for the great things He had done and the miracle He would perform for her. After singing for some time, they prayed together, and then Bob left.

The following week, this lady went for her medical checkup, and the test results showed that she was cancer-free! All the cancer cells had melted away when they were singing and praising God!

Sing Praises to God

The children of Israel knew that Jericho was part of the inheritance God had promised them. There was a big problem, though—to take Jericho, they had to bring down the walls of the city.

The Bible records that the walls surrounding Jericho were so massive that no army, however strong, could bring them down. The Israelites knew that God had given them the city, but one thing stood between them and Jericho—the walls.

Not knowing what to do, they turned to God, and He instructed them to march round Jericho for seven days. On the seventh day, they praised God with the sound of trumpets and "the people shouted with a great shout"—and the walls of Jericho came crushing down! Just like that!

Could it be, that the only thing holding you back from getting your breakthrough is a lack of praise? Praise releases the power of God in your life. It disarms the devil and arms us against the attacks of the evil one. That is how important praising God is!

Jane and her husband had been married for seven years, and they were still childless. She had gone from one gynecologist to another, trying desperately to conceive, but to no avail.

She grew to hate the sight of her own blood. Every time she had her monthly period, she would cry her eyes out. Her inability to have a baby preyed on her mind so much that she went into depression.

One day she heard about how a woman had been healed of cancer while praising God. She began to sing songs of praise and worship every day. Three months into praising and worshiping God, she became pregnant, and she is now the joyful mother of a bouncing baby boy!

Praise brings much needed joy and peace into our lives. This is the opposite of what the enemy wants for us: a life full of strain, lacking in joy and peace. It is time to take back what the devil has stolen from you; and it is possible to do exactly that, by praising and worshipping God for who He is. Praise prepares the atmosphere for God to manifest Himself; we are told that all heaven joins in when we are praising the name of our God (*Psalm 89:5*).

Yes, God is a miracle-working God. But He is also the Creator of the universe, Giver of life, and Master of all. The very reason we were created is to worship Him and Him alone. Once you do that constantly, be still and watch as He works miracle after miracle in your life!

Chapter 5

Keep a Positive Mindset

Perhaps someone somewhere once told you that you would never amount to anything in life. Maybe it was your teacher who said that you would never be able to pass a particular subject or a relative who told you that you would never get out of debt since you were such a bad financial planner.

What is frustrating is that the very people who are supposed to help us think positively of ourselves are the ones who plant seeds of doubt and uncertainty in our lives. But you do not have to let those seeds germinate and grow; cast them out at once, like the worthless weeds they are.

Whatever has been said about you is not important at all. What is more important is how you think of yourself. The only person who can write your destiny is you yourself. Do you want to be debt-free? If the answer is yes, then count it done. Do you want to overcome that addiction, enjoy good health, get a good job, or have a happy marriage? If yes, then it is as good as done!

Always encourage yourself, even when you don't have anyone around to cheer you on. True, it would be wonderful to have someone stand by you every time you are down; but if no one is forthcoming, then go ahead and motivate yourself.

Sometimes it seems as if those problems will never leave us. But if we stay in faith and believe everything will turn out well, God will make it His business to come to our rescue. It is natural for discouraging thoughts to cross your mind when troubles come, but do not let them dominate your thinking. Quickly replace negative thoughts with positive ones.

In every "hopeless" situation, create an atmosphere of faith for God to act. Perhaps you have lost your job, and you are wondering what is going to become of you and your family. You may be tempted to start worrying; but remember that anxiety will hinder God from helping you out of your problem.

You might be saying, "What is positive about losing my job?" Just remember, God has a reason for allowing it to happen. Declare your trust in Him; say boldly, "Lord, I thank you because you are working out everything for my good. I know that you have something better for me."

Keep a Positive Mindset

Negative thoughts are easy to entertain but, once they set in, it is difficult to get rid of them. They will keep replaying themselves over and over again, bringing worry and despair in their wake, and draining you of all your energy. If you allow negativity to cloud your mind, you will never see anything good come out of your circumstances.

Do not allow yourself to be held in bondage by negative thinking. Give yourself a chance to see goodness and hope in everything around you. Discipline yourself to start thinking positive, life-giving thoughts, and you will soon see how easy it is to tackle challenges with renewed energy.

You may find it hard at first to weed out all those destructive, life-draining thought patterns that have taken root over the years; but the good thing is that you can start at once to sow positive thoughts in your mind. You will become a happier person if you do so. Planting thoughts of God's provision and protection in your mind will give you peace, and you will be less easily shaken by adverse circumstances.

Perhaps you are suffering from a debilitating illness. The doctors may have given up on you, but it is not over until it is over. Do not keep telling yourself, "This illness is surely going to kill me!"

It's Not Over Yet

No, dear friend, refuse to replay that thought in your mind. Instead, declare to yourself, "I will get better every day. God is going to restore my health, and soon I will be out of this bed. I will not allow this disease to bring me down; I will trust in Jehovah Rapha, my Healer."

When you proclaim those words every day, you will start getting better and better, and those feelings of defeat and despair will disappear.

Many a time, the way we think is a direct result of our upbringing. If your family saw everything negatively, then you could have grown up thinking negatively too. On the other hand, if your family saw challenges in a positive light, then you are more likely as an adult to face life with a positive attitude. The good news, however, is that you can recondition your thoughts; you don't have to be a hostage to your past.

It does not matter what was said to you when you were young. What is more important is the here and now; if you can keep a positive mindset, little by little you will see God working in your life. Perhaps you grew up poor and everyone in your family had resigned themselves to being paupers all their lives. Perhaps someone even told you that you would never be able to get out of poverty.

Keep a Positive Mindset

Friend, rid yourself of that kind of mindset. It is not what God wants for you; He created you and deposited inside of you everything you need to overcome every single challenge that comes your way. The Bible says that no good thing will He withhold from us (*Psalm 84:11*). That is why I believe poverty is from the enemy—obviously it is not a good thing.

It is possible to overcome any kind of challenge that faces you. God says He will never allow us to be tested or tempted beyond our strength. He has assured us that, when things get really bad, He will make a way of escape for us.

> No test or temptation that comes your way is beyond the course of what others have had to face. All you need to remember is that God will never let you down; he'll never let you be pushed past your limit; he'll always be there to help you come through it.
>
> 1 Corinthians 10:13, MSG

Whatever it is that you are facing, remember to keep a positive mindset. Let God know that you still have faith in Him—that you know He will make a way out for you.

It's Not Over Yet

Negative thoughts are the root cause of complaints. The tongue utters what is already in the mind: "Oh God, why is it that I have to face this financial problem? Why did I have to get married to this person who never understands me? Why are my children so rebellious? Why, why, why!"

All these "whys" will not help you solve a single problem; instead, they will sap you of all your energy. Since God already knew everything about this problem long before it got to you, why not stop complaining and start praising God?

Tell Him, "Lord, long before it came to me, you already knew that I would have this financial problem. I thank you, Lord, because my best days are ahead of me and not behind me. I thank you that I am blessed and cannot be cursed. I know you are going to make a way out of this situation, and I am going to come out better than I was before all this happened."

Your Maker is not caught off guard by any problem facing you today. He has known about it all along and has already made a way out for you. Let Him know that you trust Him to lead you out. When you stay positive, you will have peace in any situation, and in reality you will be preparing the ground for God to manifest himself.

Keep a Positive Mindset

If God is for you, who can stand against you? As long as your ways are right with God, He will give you the strength you need to cope with anything that comes your way. Maybe it is an illness that is robbing you of your peace and joy. Perhaps you are asking yourself, "Why is it that this sickness just can't go away? Why me? Why not someone else? What did I do to deserve this?"

Friend, this kind of thinking will keep you from seeing the glory of God. Why not affirm your trust in Him? Tell Him, "Thank you that I am alive and not dead. Thank you that you are my Father and you have inscribed me on the palms of your hands. Thank you that this illness is not news to you and that it did not surprise you. I know you are Jehovah Rapha my Healer and you will come through for me. I believe you will heal me, so I am making a choice not to complain. I am making a choice to wait on you to heal me, because by your stripes I am healed."

God knows that hard times often cause our minds to play tricks on us. They will make us go off course and miss the mark. The children of Israel were in a frenzy of fear when they saw themselves trapped between the Red Sea and Pharaoh's advancing army. But Moses told them, "Do not be afraid. Stand still, and see the salvation of the Lord"

(*Exodus 14:13*). God wants us to be still and to see His salvation too. So relax and rest in His presence. Let Him show you what to do.

Perhaps you have suffered a setback. It could be a promotion you were so sure you would get, but you ended up losing it to someone who did not deserve it. Or you have been unfairly sacked from your job. Friend, if you could just say "Thank you, Father, you knew this was going to happen. I know you will make a way where there seems to be no way," you will sense peace coming into your heart.

The Bible says, "Be thankful in everything"; maybe God saw that the job you had was limiting you, and He wants to give you a better one. God has better plans for you than the ones you made for yourself. He knows why you were so unfairly judged, and the best part is that He will give you back more than what you have lost. If you will keep calm, He will show you what to do next. Just be still and wait on Him; He is the Father who loves us and is in control of everything in our lives.

A friend of mine had not seen his family for a long time. His nature of work did not allow him much free time to visit his family, who lived far away from his workplace. When he finally got the opportunity to return home to visit his family, you can imagine how happy and excited he was!

Keep a Positive Mindset

He started out early for the bus station, hoping to catch the first bus home. He did get to the bus alright but, to his surprise, the conductor would not allow him in. He told him to his face, "You will not enter this bus!"

All the other people were given seats, but not him. After some time, the vehicle filled up with passengers and left. My friend had to wait an hour for the next available bus. When it finally came, he had no problem getting on board.

As this second bus was travelling along the road, it came to the scene of an accident. My friend recognized the crashed vehicle; it was the bus that had gone ahead, the same one he had been barred from boarding. Several passengers who had been on it had died. He told me that all he could do at the time was break down in tears and thank God that the conductor was rude to him and did not allow him to board that first bus.

The next time someone mistreats you or life seems unfair to you, ask yourself: could it be that God is saving you from an accident, as He did this friend of mine? Could it be that He is saving you from making a huge mistake that could have cost you your life?

It's Not Over Yet

Friend, if you will keep in mind that He is an all-knowing God who loves you and wants the best for you, you will have no difficulty trusting Him. Your trust in Him is paramount in your walk with Him. Thank Him for everything in your life, and allow Him to work through you for His glory.

The situation you are in now is exactly where God wants you to be; this may sound crazy to you, but it is the truth. Sometimes God allows us to go through rough patches so that He can work on our faith, mold us, and teach us some life lessons. You may not know what these lessons are until you pass through whatever you are passing through. If God had not wanted you to face those challenges, He would not have allowed them to happen. Wait patiently on God, and let Him show you what He wants you to see in the midst of all your problems.

In *Psalm 23:4*, David said, "Yea, though I walk through the valley of the shadow of death, I will fear no evil; for you are with me." Though he was a very successful king, David had his own share of problems. God called him a man after His own heart (*1 Samuel 13:14*), and what made David stand out was his trust in God, even in the face of death—as when he was facing Goliath (*1 Samuel 17*) and when King Saul was pursuing him (*1 Samuel 24*).

Keep a Positive Mindset

God has promised He would always be with us and He would protect us from every calamity that threatens to overwhelm or destroy us. He has promised to make a way for us where there was no way before, and to make rivers flow in the desert; to flatten every mountain and fill up every valley, just so we can pass through. There is no obstacle too big for God to remove for you, nothing too impossible for Him to accomplish for you.

> "Fear not, for I have redeemed you;
> I have called you by your name; you are mine.
> When you pass through the waters,
>   I will be with you;
> And through the rivers,
>   they shall not overflow you.
> When you walk through the fire,
>   you shall not be burned,
> Nor shall the flame scorch you.
>
> Isaiah 43:1-2

> Behold, I will do a new thing,
> Now it shall spring forth;
> Shall you not know it?
> I will even make a road in the wilderness
> And rivers in the desert.
>
> Isaiah 43:19

It's Not Over Yet

Do not think any less of yourself, simply because you have failed a major exam or made a costly mistake. You can still pick up the pieces and move on. Do not dwell too much on the past. Just learn from your past mistakes and try not to repeat them.

Who says you can't make it in life because you come from a family that has been paupers for generations? Who says you can't become famous because you are from an obscure family and nobody knows you exist? Have a warrior mindset; know that you can do anything you have set your mind to. You can be anything you want to be.

Make friends with people who are positive thinkers. There is nothing worse than being surrounded by naysayers when you are at the lowest point. Those kinds of "friends" do not add value to your life. The best you can do is stay away from them. Instead of building you up, they will completely destroy you!

Imagine that you are drowning and you have just one chance to save yourself—if only the person you went swimming with would hand you a life buoy. You scream and yell, pleading for a life belt. But your friend just looks at you and says, "I don't think this life belt will do you any good. You were meant to die, so accept your fate."

Keep a Positive Mindset

Would you want to be anywhere near such a person? Someone who will not save your life? Definitely not! Negative people are life-draining; they sap the energy out of you. They do not help you solve problems; on the contrary, they add to whatever problems you have. They are simply a cancer you need to stay away from. You need to surround yourself instead with people who will encourage you and help you grow in your faith. People who will comfort you and tell you that nothing lasts forever, that this too shall pass…

Your mind is a battlefield, a place where all sorts of thoughts wage war against one another. In a battle, only the smartest survive, only the well-trained and well-equipped army wins. When you train your mind to think positive thoughts, you will be mentally prepared to overcome all challenges.

Who told you that success is only for others and not for you? God created you as well as those others, didn't He? The God who made the most successful person on earth is the same God who created you. If only you will keep a positive mindset and believe you are able to accomplish anything in life, then God Himself will fight your battles for you, and you will see yourself moving from one success to another.

Chapter 6

Be Joyful Always

We should never allow problems and setbacks to steal our joy. In the midst of all the difficulties you are going through, remember to keep your joy. The Bible says it clearly: rejoice always. It does not say you are to rejoice only when things are going your way; it says to rejoice *always*:

> Rejoice in the Lord always:
> And again I say, Rejoice.
> *Philippians 4:4, KJV*

> Rejoice always, pray without ceasing, in everything give thanks; for this is the will of God in Christ Jesus for you.
> *1 Thessalonians 5:16-18*

It may seem unreal, even crazy, to rejoice when you have lost your job, and you do not know what to do next: when you do not know where your next meal is coming from; or when your child has dropped out of school because you could not afford to pay the fees. You wonder just how possible it is to be joyful in such circumstances.

Be Joyful Always

Is it possible to rejoice and not give in to fear or despair in all circumstances? Yes! The Bible shows us how:

> Do not be anxious about anything, but in every situation, by prayer and petition, with thanksgiving, present your requests to God. And the peace of God, which transcends all understanding, will guard your hearts and your minds in Christ Jesus.
> *Philippians 4:6-7, NIV*

Once you let God take care of your problems, you will not be anxious about anything. You will be at peace—because you know that everything will turn out well in the end. God knows the end from the beginning; and where you are right now is where He wants you to be. It is not a mistake that you lost your job—He knows why. When you are aware that God has you in the palms of His hands, that He has the best plan for your life, and that He is directing your steps, you will be able to rejoice.

Give your burdens to God, and He will restore your joy. For He has said, "Cast your burden on the Lord, and He shall sustain you" (*Psalm 55:22*); and, again, "Cast all your anxiety on him because he cares for you" (*1 Peter 5:7, NIV*).

It's Not Over Yet

Stay in faith; do not let your heart be troubled, but constantly remind yourself that your Heavenly Father is watching over you at all times. Indeed, He who watches over you will neither slumber nor sleep (*Psalm 121:4*). He will keep you from all harm (*Psalm 121:7*). He is aware of every move you make, and He will watch over your coming and going, both now and forevermore (*Psalm 121:8, NIV*).

What makes me happy all the time is knowing that God already has a way out for every single one of my problems, no matter how big they seem. This makes me depend on God and trust Him even more. I wake up every morning with an expectant heart, convinced beyond a shadow of a doubt that I am a child of God and that He loves me so much He will solve whatever problem comes my way. The bigger the problem, the greater the miracle. All I have to do is to let my Heavenly Father take my problems and solve them for me.

The steps of a righteous man are ordered by the LORD (*Psalm 37:23*). God is never caught by surprise; before you even encounter any of these problems, He already has the solution to them. If you stay on the highway on faith and keep trusting in God, you will see Him make a way where there seems to be no way.

Be Joyful Always

He said that He will make a way in the wilderness and rivers in the desert (*Isaiah 43:19-20; 41:18*). Your financial barrenness is nothing to Him. Note: He says He will make rivers spring forth *in* the desert; He does not say He will take you *out* of the desert.

He will give you a new idea that will revive your struggling business. He will open another door for you to get a better-paid job. He will give you grace to endure when you have lost a loved one. He will take care of you, no matter what happens to you. The enemy is under your feet as long as you stay on the highway of faith.

God sometimes puts us in the wilderness for a purpose. Perhaps He wants to teach you to trust Him more or to reveal certain heavenly secrets to you. Maybe He wants to straighten out a particular area in your life where He sees a weakness. The good news is that, when God allows you to go through hardship, He does not abandon you; instead, He is always there to help you. You just have to call on His name.

Times may be tough, but that is not reason enough to live a miserable life. Get up, dig in your heels, and make a decision to rejoice always, no matter what happens. God has got you covered.

It's Not Over Yet

When you keep a happy and thankful attitude, you are also more likely to find a solution to your problems. This is because we tend to think more clearly when we stay calm and focused. You will be able to hear God's still, small voice telling you what to do. But, when you get yourself all worked up, you will only end up worried, frustrated and defeated. There is no way you can get anything done in that condition, and you will be stuck with your problems for longer than necessary.

Worry and woe tire us out; but the joy of the LORD is our strength (*Nehemiah 8:10*). Let go of the little foxes of anxiety that drain the life out of you and leave you feeling hopeless. If you stay grumpy and unhappy, you will have no strength to continue fighting. But, if you rejoice in the Lord even in the worst of times, He will give you the strength to go on.

Paul said, "I can do all things through Christ who strengthens me" (*Philippians 4:13*). Likewise with us. So, wake up every morning with renewed energy and make a deliberate decision to stay joyful no matter what happens. Make it your mission to improve your life. If you are in a financial crisis, make every effort to get out of it. Nothing is impossible, if only you can believe.

Be Joyful Always

Perhaps you are not able to rejoice because you are still holding a grudge against someone who has wronged you. For instance, a colleague might have backstabbed you at your workplace and, in one way or another, caused you to lose your job. You need to forgive and let go of this person; this will help you lead a happy and fulfilled life.

Or perhaps you have been deeply hurt by someone's cutting words. People who put you down, who sit in judgment over you, who predict a bleak future for you—their remarks can easily steal your joy. Do not listen to them. Do not even get angry with them or hold any grudge against them. The best thing you can do for yourself is to forgive them. Let it go and move on.

In most cases, when people speak badly about you, it is because they see something good in you that they do not have, and so they envy you. Bless them, and do not allow them to steal your joy. Be happy that you are who you are.

What anyone says about you is really not important. What is important is what you think about yourself. It could be that you are down today; things have not been going your way lately. But this is no reason for you to lose your joy or to think any less of yourself.

It's Not Over Yet

Yes, you may have made mistakes. You may be where you are now because of wrong decisions you made previously. But nobody needs to rub it; nobody needs to remind you of past blunders. Do not allow anyone to harp on how many errors you have made in the past.

Review your life, identify why you are in that crisis. Could it be because of wrong choices you made? Or because of the bad company you kept? The so-called "friends" who did you more harm than good? It does not really matter; give yourself a break. It's a new day, a new beginning. Hold on to your zeal to change things for the better.

If you have made a choice to rectify your life, just move on. Let the past stay in the past. You can pick up the pieces and start all over again. Learn from past mistakes but do not dwell on what might have been, it will not help you; instead, it will stop you from moving forward. You will not be able to plan ahead if you are still holding onto the past.

Let nothing ever steal your happiness. Let bygones be bygones. Sure, you made some poor choices, but don't let yourself dwell there. Nobody is perfect; we all make mistakes, but dwelling on our past will hinder our growth. It will make us constantly frustrated and depressed.

Be Joyful Always

When you were making that mistake, you thought it was the right thing to do at that particular moment. Well, now that you know where you went wrong, you can do it right this time round. There is no reason to wallow in self-pity. Life offers us many chances to turn ourselves around.

Stop listening to people who say negative things to you; their destructive words can make you lose hope and feel like a failure. Keep away from them and do not go around asking what they have said about you either. Ignore them.

If you open your ears to negative people, be warned that whatever they say will completely take away your joy. Eventually you will become resentful and bitter towards them, which is not at all healthy. It is better to walk away from them. Vicious words are like pure poison; they will surely kill you in the end.

You may be tempted to believe them when they say that you will never make it. But if you allow that kind of mindset to creep in, you will be letting in venom that will eventually destroy you. When such comments come your way, just ignore them. Declare to yourself that the joy of the Lord is your strength and your portion forever.

It's Not Over Yet

True joy comes from God, and we should learn to seek God for it. The joy of the Lord helps us see our circumstances in a different way—His way. The joy of the Lord will enable you to thank God in all circumstances, being assured that He is in control of everything in your life. And, by doing so, new doors will open for you, because God has said in His Word that He delights in the thanksgiving of His people.

The devil comes only to steal, kill and destroy (*John 10:10*). His objective is to steal our joy, to make sure we go around feeling hopeless, unhappy and defeated. Do not give him that pleasure. When the enemy makes you feel like you are all alone, remember there is One who will never leave you (*Hebrews 13:5*). Even when you are in the desert and nothing seems to work, God has promised that He will always be there for you.

When the devil is coming against you, and you feel helpless, discouraged and frustrated, that is the time to remind God that He has said He will repay double for every unfair thing done against you (*Isaiah 61:7; Zechariah 9:12*). Claim His promises. Our God is a faithful God; what He has said He will do. He will surely make it come to pass.

Be Joyful Always

Isn't it a blessing to know that we have a Father who takes care of everything for us, just so we can live a joyful, fulfilled life? Don't go around grumpy and miserable because things are not going your way. Put a smile on your face and let God have your problems. Let Him show you His goodness and you won't regret it.

Each morning brings its own challenges, but they should not spoil your day. Learn to go with the flow. When your plans do not work out the way you expected them to, that is no reason for you to go through the day all depressed and stressed out. Remember that nothing happens unless God has allowed it to.

Life is too short to spend fretting over situations that are beyond your control, and making yourself and everyone around you miserable. Make a deliberate decision today to stay happy; tell yourself, "I am going to keep my joy even if I did not get that job or date or whatever it is that I so desperately wanted. I am going to enjoy my life today, no matter what happens!"

Chapter 7

Belief Backed by Action Is Powerful

The Bible tells us that, when we pray, we should believe that we *already* have what we ask for:

> Therefore I tell you, whatever you ask for in prayer, believe that you have received it, and it will be yours.
>
> *Mark 11:24, NIV*

It is one thing to ask God to heal you, mend your relationships with loved ones, or give you financial breakthroughs; but it is another thing to believe that you *already* have what you are praying for. This is where the challenge comes in—*believing that you already have it*.

Friend, it is alright to plead incessantly with God to help you. But, if you do not go one step further and believe that you are improving day by day, your rebellious child is being transformed, your marriage is getting better, then it will take a long time to have things turn around for you.

Belief Backed by Action Is Powerful

God has already done His part. The moment you knelt down and prayed, God answered your prayer; but you cannot receive your miracle unless you believe in it.

The moment you concentrate on the problem and not the solution, you will lose God's blessings. If you focus on how big your problem is—how your marriage cannot be salvaged, how your financial crisis is so bad, or how you are so much in debt that nothing seems to work—you are not going to see miracles happening in your life.

Believe that you are able to maintain good relationships with your family; believe that you are going to have the child that you long for; believe that you are going to get out of financial difficulties. When you do that, God gets moving on your behalf, and soon you will see things changing in your favor.

When Jesus was healing the sick, He would ask, "Do you believe I can help you?" What He means is that you have to completely believe it will happen. Even if it seems impossible, do not give way to doubts; keep on believing that what you are looking for is coming your way. Our God is more than able to do exceedingly abundantly above all we ask Him to do for us (*Ephesians 3:20*).

It's Not Over Yet

It is possible to miss your destiny by a whisker because it seems too much to hope for. We tend to see things with our carnal eyes and reason with our carnal mind; as a result, we miss the great things God has in store for us.

You may have come from a long family line of failures; but where you come from does not necessarily determine who you are or where you are going. If God has put in you a dream to be the first successful doctor, architect, entrepreneur or inventor in your family, by all means go for it. Believe that you can rise above the status quo. Be the one who will break that cycle of poverty and failure in your family. Purpose in your heart that nothing can stand between you and your destiny.

Negative thoughts will cross your mind from time to time. But do not give credence to them. Do not let them put doubt in your heart. Have faith in God; put your total trust in your Creator. You are what He says you are: a victor, not a victim. In all things, believe you are more than a conqueror through Him who loves you (*Romans 8:37*).

It is amazing how seriously God takes unbelief. It was the Israelites' unbelief that angered God. Because of their unbelief, they died in the wilderness and did not enter the Promised Land.

Belief Backed by Action Is Powerful

> Now with whom was He angry forty years? Was it not with those who sinned, whose corpses fell in the wilderness? And to whom did He swear that they would not enter His rest, but to those who did not obey? So we see that they could not enter in because of unbelief.
>
> *Hebrews 3: 17-19*

Despite all the miracles God had done to deliver them from slavery in Egypt, the Israelites did not believe Him when He told them He was going to bring them into a land flowing with milk and honey. As a result, they never got to see the Promised Land.

Unbelief can also cause us to miss the good things God has in store for us. But if we keep on believing that God has already given us all He has promised us, we will find everything working out in our favor. When you entrust your life entirely to God, He will guide you to your destiny.

Have an expectant heart, wake up every morning expecting more of God's love, more of His favor. Lift your head high and declare, "I am blessed, I can do all things through Christ who strengthens me, I am more than a conqueror, nothing can faze me."

It's Not Over Yet

The Bible says that faith without action is dead (*James 2:14-26*). Many a time, we say we do believe; but our actions show otherwise. Trying to pray your way out of your problem is not enough; you have to put some action behind your faith.

Many times, we pray to God to help us. We cry, "Oh God, help me get out of this financial crisis. Give me a job. Help me get married. Give me a child. Help me get well. Heal my marriage, my relationships..." but we fail to realize that we have to do our part too.

Don't just pray and wait for God to give you things on a silver platter. Nothing will fall from heaven. You need to get up and do something about your situation. If you are jobless, start looking for a job and let God's favor guide you. If you are sick, and you are serious about getting better, start making plans to live a healthy life. Get some exercise and stop eating junk food.

The doctors may have given you a bad report and told you that you have a very serious health condition. Do not start making plans on how you will die. Instead, start declaring that you will improve, that each day you are getting better and better. It does not matter how serious the situation is. As long as there is hope, never give in to defeat.

BELIEF BACKED BY ACTION IS POWERFUL

Perhaps you have been told your health is not looking good at all. The doctors may have given you a bad medical report and told you that you have a life-threatening illness. Do not start making plans for your funeral, but keep declaring that you will improve and that you are getting better and better each day.

Start declaring God's promises to yourself: "With long life He will satisfy me" (*Psalm 91:16*). But don't just pray; start doing what you were told you would not be able to do. If they said that you would not be able to walk again, start exercising your legs; put some action behind that faith. Let God give you the strength you need.

If you are praying to get out of debt, start managing your finances better. Do not buy just about everything you come across. If you spend your money on designer clothes that you really do not need or a new pair of shoes, just because you think they are fashionable, then you are acting in direct opposition to your prayers.

It is possible to live a debt-free life. Just be more careful in your spending. Stop buying things on impulse. Buy only the things you really need and pay for them in cash. Resist the urge to use your credit cards. Soon you will realize that you can do it; you can enjoy life and not worry about finances.

It's Not Over Yet

Do not go through life feeling defeated. God has good things in store for you, if only you will believe and act on your beliefs. If God has put a dream in your heart and you have a strong conviction that it is what He wants you to do—go for it. Do not waste time talking yourself out of it by looking at the obstacles.

Do not doubt for a second that you are able to do what God has put in your heart. If He did put His dream in your heart, it is because He knows you are able to achieve it. Maybe God has called you to write a book, and you are asking yourself, "How on earth is it possible for an ordinary person like me to do that?"

Friend, the people who have written books started just like you. They were unknown before they wrote their first books; yet they believed in themselves, took a step of faith, and are where they are today because they put their faith in action.

Do not give negative thoughts a chance to ruin your day or destroy your dream. Tell your Heavenly Father, "I know that you are a faithful God, you have promised never to leave me nor forsake me. Now help me to attain this goal!" When you do that, you will gain new strength to pursue your dream.

Belief Backed by Action Is Powerful

God has promised us that, when we tell Him our plans, He will direct our paths (*Proverbs 3:6*). He will make our paths straight; He will level the mountains and fill the valleys, just to make sure you have a clear way to get to where you want to be.

Sometimes, to get on the right track to your destiny, you may have to ignore negative comments. You may have to go against discouraging, unproductive "advice" from the very people you love—but, in the end, it will be worth the discipline it took to do that.

Remember, the dream was born in you, not in them. The calling to write a book was born in you and not in anyone else. It therefore does not matter what everyone else says. Stop talking about it and just do it—start writing!

Take time to review your life. What is it that is limiting you from becoming God's best? What is it you are doing that is keeping you from achieving your dream? Find out what is holding you back from succeeding, deal with it, and let God make the best out of you.

Maybe you are so grumpy that people fear being around you. Start making positive changes in your life. Start smiling more often. Start being friendly to people, and they will reciprocate. Soon they will find it fun to be around you.

It's Not Over Yet

Maybe you have reviewed your life and dealt with your shortcomings, and still nothing seems to work. You are still without a job; your health is still not improving; but that is not a license to doubt God. Stay in faith; wake up every morning expecting someone to call you and offer you the job you want; or your doctor to tell you that the tumor he thought was malignant turned out to be harmless after all.

Expect good and not evil. Expect God to enlarge your borders; expect Him to heal you; expect Him to mend your broken relationships. When you do that, you will not go through the day all grumpy and frustrated—no! Your heart will be filled with joy, and you will be smiling and expecting something good to come your way.

Take, for example, a pregnant woman who is expecting the birth of her child soon. She will definitely make plans for it. She will decide on the hospital to go to for the delivery; she will buy baby clothes, get the crib, and decorate the nursery so that everything is ready for the newborn.

Have the same expectant spirit inside of you. Make plans for what you are expecting. If it is a new car you are expecting God to bless you with, go to the dealer, get to know everything about that car, then work towards achieving your dream.

Belief Backed by Action Is Powerful

I have a friend who came from a very poor background. She told me that having three square meals a day was a miracle back then. She did not have a bank account, but she would go to a bank, queue up with all the other people who were waiting to be attended to, and pretend that she too had an account with the bank.

While waiting in the queue, she would whisper a prayer and ask God to remember her. It was not long before she got a well-paying job and was able to open an account with that bank. Now, that is faith in action!

Start acting on God's promises in His Word. Confess them with your mouth. When we act on God's Word, when we act in faith, we get His attention. God rewards those who believe in Him (*Hebrews 11:6*). If we diligently seek Him and keep expecting from Him, He will fill our baskets with good things. He has promised that no good thing will He ever withhold from us (*Psalm 84:11*). Hold Him to that!

When you get up each morning, thank God for what He is going to do for you. Expect to get that promotion, even if you know that your colleagues are more qualified than you are. Expect to hold that baby in your arms, even if the doctors are saying that you will not be able to conceive.

It's Not Over Yet

Visualize your family living in that beautiful dream house, even if you do not have a dollar to your name. Put some action behind your faith. Start planning for the baby you want, even if you are not pregnant yet. Start window shopping for new furniture for your dream house.

Do not limit yourself to where you are right now. Get a bigger dream, a bigger goal, and expect God to help you achieve those dreams and goals, no matter how impossible it seems. Do not talk yourself out of the good, fulfilling life that God wants you to have. Go ahead and do what you want to do. Take deliberate steps towards achieving your goal.

Sometimes, all we need in life is a little push. Just an encouraging word said to you—and something is sparked off inside. You feel nothing can stop you. You feel you can do anything. And when you take action, you will discover that the world is full of opportunities.

Chapter 8

Learn to Forgive

It is true that we sometimes face problems because someone somewhere was unfair to us. Maybe you lost your job because a colleague framed you for things you did not do. Perhaps you were doing well at work, and people became envious and told the boss horrible lies about you, out of sheer jealousy. Or perhaps your subordinate wanted your position and thought the only way to get it was to get rid of you.

Yes, it leaves a bitter taste in the mouth just to think of it—that people you trusted would stab you in the back just so they could see you out of a job. But, friend, when something like this happens, always remember you are not alone. God has promised never to leave you or forsake you.

Even though it is hard to do, hold your head up high. Forgive the person who cost you that job. God has promised that He will repay you double for every unfair thing done to you. He has not forgotten what you went through. He was there when they were bad-mouthing you.

IT'S NOT OVER YET

Friend, just forgive those people; let God be your vindicator. He knows everything that happened to you, how it happened, and why it happened. Losing your job does not mean that you won't get another one. God is more than able to give you a better-paying job in a better company with a better boss. But this will only happen if you forgive those who have hurt you.

When bad things happen to us because of what people have done, we tend to hold grudges against them. We become bitter and resentful. We wonder, "Why me?" We ask ourselves why God allowed those things to happen while He was keeping watch over us. If this is what you are doing now, quit asking yourself all those questions. They will only make you feel worse than you already do.

Nothing happens behind God's back; He knew what they were plotting to do, and He allowed it to happen. Our circumstances do not change who God is in our lives; so honor Him by forgiving your adversary. It is not worth it, to keep a heavy heart because someone was unfair to you.

Do not let bitterness cloud your mind so much that, every time you hear the name of the person who wronged you, your heart skips a beat; you will end up having hypertension for nothing.

Learn to Forgive

If you keep bitterness in your heart, you will be playing into the enemy's hands. The devil will then have legal grounds to operate in your life, thereby causing you even more harm. Do not allow the enemy to take over the affairs of your life so easily.

If you remain unforgiving, you will be opening your door to all sorts of demonic attacks. If you think losing your job is bad, you haven't seen anything yet! Close that door immediately by asking God to help you forgive your enemies.

There is no way you can serve two masters; either you are serving God or the enemy. When you are unforgiving and bitter, you are a perfect servant of the devil. Friend, quit being the enemy's slave; it is not worth it.

Yes, it is hard to forgive people who have wronged you and caused you so much pain; but in the end it is your life that is important. Thank God that they took your job and not your life. Thank God that you are healthy. Keep thanking God for every single thing in your life.

Let your vision guide you into greater achievements. It does not matter what has been said about you. It really isn't important whether anyone believes in you. As long as God is on your side, nothing else matters.

It's Not Over Yet

Remember, the people who put you in that situation wanted to make you miserable; and, by becoming bitter, you are helping them to attain their objective. By being unforgiving, you are giving them the pleasure of ruining your dream. You are letting them stop you from reaching your destiny. But, when you forgive them, God is able to work His miracles in your life.

If you can learn to forgive your enemies, you will discover that things become much easier on your side. Once you have repented before God for being unforgiving, tell Him you have completely forgiven those who hurt you. Continuously confess aloud with your mouth that you have forgiven them. When you do that, a heavy weight will be taken off your shoulders; you will have closed the door upon the enemy and opened the door for God to fight for you.

A Christian woman became paralyzed after falling down from a tractor. She was hospitalized for months, but her husband never visited her. What's more, he went ahead and married another woman. And, to add insult to injury, her husband told their children that their mother had died—and that was why he was marrying another wife!

Learn to Forgive

Month after month, she was in the hospital. Nobody visited her except for a lady friend. One day the hospital staff told her they could not keep her anymore; she was free to go home. Her heart broke because she had no home to go to. She requested her friend to take her to a church so that she could seek refuge there.

The pastor allowed the paralyzed woman to stay in the church, but there was a problem: the room she was given was upstairs. The church was built in such a way that the sanctuary was on the ground floor and the guestroom was upstairs; so they had to carry her up the stairs to her room.

She stayed in that church for some time with her friend, who was on hand to help her whenever she needed to go to the bathroom. After a while, the two ladies decided to fast and pray day and night for her healing. On the seventh night of fasting, while her friend dozed off, the paralyzed woman continued to pray and plead with God to heal her.

Suddenly she heard an audible voice asking her if she wanted to be made whole again. She said yes. The voice said that, if she wanted to be healed, she had to forgive those who had hurt her, especially her husband and the lady he married. There and then, the lady agreed to forgive them completely.

It's Not Over Yet

The voice then told her to stand. She replied that she was unable to do so. Then she felt a hand holding her up and helping her to stand. Immediately, she felt strength flowing through her body, and she was able to walk! She ran down the stairs, shouting her thanks to God for healing her.

You can imagine how happy she was! But note that God told her she could not receive any healing until she forgave the people who had hurt her.

There are no two ways about it: for you to receive your miracle, you must forgive those who have hurt you. If you are finding it hard to forgive them, ask God to help you. Forgiving your enemies will give you the courage to go before God in prayer and ask Him for mercy for yourself.

Jesus tells us that, if we forgive those who sin against us, our heavenly Father will also forgive us; but, if we refuse to forgive them, God will not forgive us our sins either (*Matthew 6:14-15; Matthew 18:21-35; Mark 11:25-26*).

> For if you forgive other people when they sin against you, your heavenly Father will also forgive you. But if you do not forgive others their sins, your Father will not forgive your sins.
>
> *Matthew 6:14-15, NIV*

Learn to Forgive

When we forgive others, we will have grounds to go before the Creator of the universe to ask Him to fight our battles for us. But, where we withhold forgiveness from others, we will receive none from God for ourselves.

The one who said "to forgive is divine" was certainly right; it takes God's grace to let go of the wrongdoing that could have cost you your life. But it is well worth it. At the end of it all, let us always remember that we are a peculiar people, called out of darkness into God's marvelous light (*Titus 2:14; 1 Peter 2:9, KJV*); we are God's chosen people, and we have to be like Him, extending mercy to others. After all, how different are you from your enemies, if you do not forgive them?

Thank God for what you still have, instead of dwelling on what was taken away from you. Come to think of it, the very fact that you are reading this book means that you are alive—and that is one thing to thank God for!

Do not take your life for granted. It is a gift to be alive. It is a gift to be healthy. It is a gift to have a wonderful friend, spouse or family who supports you. Friend, do not dwell on the past; it will leave you all bitter and depressed. Learn to thank God for every single thing that He has done for you.

It's Not Over Yet

The fact that you are facing a tough time only means it is an opportunity for God to show you His favor and shower you with His blessings. When God shuts one door, it only means that He is about to open another for you. When He takes you from one place, it only means that He is about to bring you to a better one—a place where you will reach your destiny much easier and faster.

Focus on God's faithfulness and mercy. Rest assured that you have His approval, and that is all that matters. Let go of all the baggage you have; release yourself from all of it, and get ready to go higher.

The best part about all this is that God is in control. So let peace be your friend. If you live your life full of peace, things will be much easier to handle. Despite everything that is happening, despite what our enemies are planning against us, we still have the approval of the Creator of the universe. And, in reality, that is all that matters.

Chapter 9

Be Disciplined

It is important to be disciplined if you want to attain your goal. Sometimes, this may mean looking back, asking yourself why you are in that situation, and taking tough but necessary steps to solve the problem.

Maybe it is a marriage that is simply not working out. The person you are living with does not seem to be the same one you married. Now, ask yourself: why should you be feeling this way? Why are you not happy with your spouse? After all, at one point you were so in love with this person that you could have done anything for him or her. So what happened to make you feel that the two of you are not compatible anymore?

Make an effort to find out the root cause of the problem. Could it be that, somewhere along the way, you got so used to one another you didn't see the need to share secrets anymore? Could it be a breakdown in communications? Once you have identified the cause of the problem, get to work on the solution.

It's Not Over Yet

Work out a plan to revive the excitement in your marriage. Start making an effort to get along with your spouse; learn to value this important person in your life. Let your partner know that you care, and that you are always there for him or her. If you can take the time to sincerely meet the other person halfway, you will discover that life is so much more fun—and you will come to realize that your spouse is not that bad after all!

Or you could be doing fine in your marriage, but there is something else you need to work on. Maybe you want to lose weight; you want a healthier body. Well, that is a great idea, but you won't be able to do it unless you stay focused. To achieve your goal, you will need to be disciplined in sticking to your diet and daily exercise routine.

Or perhaps it is the state of your finances that is making you lose sleep. Maybe you have made some poor choices in the past that have put you in the financial crisis you are in now. If you truly desire to get out of your difficulties, you need to start making some major adjustments to your life. Start developing the habit of thrift. Some of us live paycheck-to-paycheck; by the time you get your pay, you have already planned how to use all of it—and in a week's time, you will have nothing left.

Be Disciplined

You need to learn to budget. Make a shopping list, arranging items in order of priority. Start with the basic necessities that you really need to live on, followed by those things that, though important, may not be absolutely essential. Last on the list would be luxuries that you don't really need.

You will be able to see at once, from your list, where you can save some money. You may even end up with savings left over at the end of the month; then, by all means, put that extra money away in your bank account. Soon, you will have accumulated a substantial amount of savings, and you will realize that it is so much easier to save for a rainy day than to keep borrowing from others.

The key to getting yourself out of financial difficulty is discipline. Thank God that you have an income; all you need to do is draw up a budget for yourself. Yes, you may have to forego some comforts for a while. It may be painful to deny yourself those luxuries you are so used to having; but it is worth the sacrifice in the end, when you finally find yourself debt-free.

Or, you might be saying, "Don't talk to me about being disciplined in my spending. I don't even have a job or an income to spend!" If that is the case, then your job should be to look for a job.

It's Not Over Yet

Wake up every day and prepare yourself as if you are going to work. Make it your duty to spend the whole day looking for a job. Send out your resume to every employer you know of. Never give up, even if all the companies tell you they are not hiring; soon you will hit the jackpot.

The problem when we are jobless is that, often, hopelessness sets in. You sit back and pity yourself all day. You think you have come to the end of your rope. Friend, that is a lie from the devil; you *will* make it. Let God be your guide.

Do not listen when the enemy whispers in your ear that, since you were laid off by your previous employer, you will amount to nothing. That is a big lie. God has already opened a door for you. He already has a job for you. But how will you know, unless you get up and start looking for it?

Or, perhaps life is going well for you, and you do not have any major problems to contend with. But, still, you have dreams you want to fulfill. It could be a dream house that you want to build. Again, it takes discipline to put your plan into place. You may not have the full sum of money needed yet, but with discipline and persistence, you will definitely succeed in saving up enough to build the house of your dreams.

Be Disciplined

Discipline is a major contributor to success in all spheres of life. It does not matter how big your dream is. It does not matter what kind of opposition is facing you. If you can stick to your plan and diligently follow it to the letter, you can achieve anything you want in life—anything.

Sometimes we pray earnestly to God to give us breakthroughs in various areas of our life. Now, while it is good to pray, it is also of utmost importance to do our part. Make sure you meet all the targets you have set for yourself, and on time. Life requires us to practice discipline if we want to achieve anything at all. You cannot simply pray your way to success. If you are not disciplined and not prepared to work hard, I have news for you—it just won't work.

Sometimes, too, the wrong kind of friends may cause you to lose your focus; so you need to be careful who you associate with. Needless to say, some friends and relatives are a great inspiration to us, and we should thank God for them. However, there may be others who are more of a hindrance than a help to us, especially when we are trying to make it in life. In fact, some of these "friends" may actually turn against you when you share your dreams with them.

It's Not Over Yet

When this happens, remember to keep your focus steadfastly on the vision you have set before you. Let it be your roadmap, guiding you to where you want to be in the coming years of your life. As for those people who are trying to talk you out of your dream, do not be anywhere around them; it is not worth it.

Yes, it can be painful to let go of "friends" you have known for a long time. But, if they are holding you back from becoming all you want to be, you will definitely be better off without them. They could have been great people before. They may even have helped you previously. But that is not reason enough to hold onto them now. Their season for being in your life is gone; it is a new season for you, and in this new season you have no alternative but to move on.

Review the friends you have now. If any of them are contributing to your stagnation, then they have no business being in your life. Shake them off. Surround yourself instead with people who speak faith and sleep faith. You need to be disciplined about this, even if it feels like it is killing you to let go of your old friends. Be assured that, when you do this, God will bring new friends into your life — friends who will lift you up, not drag you down.

Be Disciplined

We should also discipline ourselves to think positively at all times. If you are used to thinking negatively, it can be really hard at first to replace those negative thoughts with positive ones. But if you persist, little by little, you will find your thought life changing.

You will become a happier, more confident person as you get into the habit of expecting good things to come to you every day. You will wake up every morning with an expectant heart, secure in the knowledge that God is in control of your life and something wonderful is coming your way.

Remember, too, that the power of life and death is in your tongue. Train your tongue to bless yourself and those around you. The moment you discipline yourself by carefully weighing what comes out of your mouth, you will be preparing the ground for God to work supernaturally in your life.

Be disciplined, too, in constantly thanking God. Sometimes, when we do not get what we want, we complain so much that we forget to thank God for all that He has already given us. Deliberately identify the things God has already done for you, and keep thanking Him for them. Develop the habit, too, of thanking Him in advance for all that you are asking Him to do for you.

It's Not Over Yet

Friend, this life is a battlefield. It is not just a minor skirmish; it is a major war that you will either win or lose. When you speak good things about yourself, about your children, about your family, and when you praise and thank God for the good things He has done for you, you are actually winning the war against the enemy. Little by little, you will see everything turning around in your favor.

Finally, it is most important to discipline yourself to read the Word of God every day. The Bible says that faith comes by hearing the word of God (*Romans 10:17*); let the enemy know that you are aware of God's promises in every situation that you face.

Do not be short on God's Word when facing any situation in your life. You do not have to read a whole chapter every day, if it seems too daunting a task at first; start with just one or two verses a day. If you can discipline yourself to read a small portion of Scripture every single day, you will not be short on ammunition to fight against the enemy when a dark day strikes.

Remember, the devil also knows the Word of God. If he could quote Scripture to tempt Jesus, you can imagine how much more he will test you.

Then Jesus was led up by the Spirit into the wilderness to be tempted by the devil. And when He had fasted forty days and forty nights, afterward He was hungry.

Now when the tempter came to Him, he said, "If You are the Son of God, command that these stones become bread."

But He answered and said, *"It is written*, 'Man shall not live by bread alone, but by every word that proceeds from the mouth of God.'"

Then the devil took Him up into the holy city, set Him on the pinnacle of the temple, and said to Him, "If You are the Son of God, throw Yourself down. For it is written:

'He shall give His angels charge over you,'

and,

'In their hands they shall bear you up, lest you dash your foot against a stone.'"

Jesus said to him, *"It is written again*, 'You shall not tempt the Lord your God.'"

Again, the devil took Him up on an exceedingly high mountain, and showed Him all the kingdoms of the world and their glory. And he said to Him, "All these things I will give You if You will fall down and worship me."

It's Not Over Yet

> Then Jesus said to him, "Away with you, Satan! For *it is written*, 'You shall worship the Lord your God, and Him only you shall serve.'"
> Then the devil left Him, and behold, angels came and ministered to Him.
> *Matthew 4:1-11*

Be filled with the knowledge of God's Word so that you can tell the devil where to get off, just as Jesus did. You should be able to tell the enemy:

"IT IS WRITTEN!"

"GOD SAID IT, I BELIEVE IT,
AND THAT'S ALL THERE IS TO IT!"

www.ingramcontent.com/pod-product-compliance
Lightning Source LLC
Chambersburg PA
CBHW060817050426
42449CB00008B/1707